P9-CMA-346

BLAIRSVILLE SENIOR HIGH SCHOOL
BLAIRSVILLE, PENNA

NASCAR Chase for the Cup

Gail Blasser Riley
AR B.L.: 2.9
Points: 0.5   MG

The World of NASCAR

NASCAR Chase for the Cup

by Gail Blasser Riley

Reading Consultant:
Barbara J. Fox
Reading Specialist
North Carolina State University

Content Consultant:
Betty L. Carlan
Research Librarian
International Motorsports Hall of Fame
Talladega, Alabama

Capstone press®

Mankato, Minnesota

T 13352 NASCAR Chase for the Cup Riley, Gail Blasser.

Blazers is published by Capstone Press,
151 Good Counsel Drive, P.O. Box 669, Mankato, Minnesota 56002.
www.capstonepress.com

Copyright © 2008 by Capstone Press, a Capstone Publishers company.
All rights reserved.
No part of this publication may be reproduced in whole or in part,
or stored in a retrieval system, or transmitted in any form or by any means,
electronic, mechanical, photocopying, recording, or otherwise,
without written permission of the publisher.
For information regarding permission, write to Capstone Press,
151 Good Counsel Drive, P.O. Box 669, Dept. R, Mankato, Minnesota 56002.
Printed in the United States of America

Library of Congress Cataloging-in-Publication Data
Riley, Gail Blasser.
    NASCAR Chase for the Cup / by Gail Blasser Riley.
    p. cm. — (Blazers. The World of NASCAR)
    Includes bibliographical references and index.
    ISBN-13: 978-1-4296-1285-2 (hardcover)
    ISBN-10: 1-4296-1285-1 (hardcover)
    1. Stock car racing — United States — Juvenile literature. 2. NASCAR
Chase for the Sprint Cup — Juvenile literature. 3. NASCAR (Association) —
Juvenile literature. I. Title. II. Series.
GV1029.9.S74R545 2008
796.72 — dc22   2007029967

Summary: Describes the racing format of the Chase for the Sprint Cup
    including its history and cup records.

Essential content terms are **bold** and are defined on the spread where they
first appear.

Editorial Credits
Mandy Robbins, editor; Bobbi J. Wyss, designer; Jo Miller, photo researcher

Photo Credits
AP Images/Chris Gardner, 20; Darron Cummings, 15; Terry Renna, 18–19, 24;
    Paul Vathas, 27
Corbis/Sam Sharpe, 7
Getty Images for NASCAR/ Chris Graythen, cover; Chris Trotman, 11; Jerry
    Markland, 28; Jonathan Ferrey, 6; Michael Brown, 22; Rusty Jarrett, 8–9;
    Getty Images, Inc./Allsport/David Taylor, 26; Nick Laham, 21; Time Life
    Pictures/Grey Villet, 16
The Sharpe Image/Sam Sharpe, 5
ZUMA Press/Sporting News/Harold Hinson, 12–13

The publisher does not endorse products whose logos may appear on
objects in images in this book.

1 2 3 4 5 6 13 12 11 10 09 08

Table of Contents

Race to the Chase

The Chevy Rock and Roll 400 was the last regular season race of 2006. It was a big race for Tony Stewart and Kasey Kahne. Both drivers had to do well to be in the Chase for the Cup.

5

Stewart was the 2005 winner. He was eighth in the points standings. But a bad **qualifying** run put him at the back of the pack. Through the race, he struggled to pull ahead of the other cars.

Tony Stewart

qualify — to earn a starting spot in a race by completing timed laps

Before the race, Kahne was 11th in the points standings. But he started the race in the front half of the pack. This put him ahead of Stewart in points. Kahne had to keep it that way.

Kasey Kahne, front row left

When the checkered flag waved, Kahne was in third place. He finished far ahead of Stewart. Fans were shocked. Kahne had knocked last year's champ out of the Chase for the Cup.

TRACK FACT!

Before 2007, only the top 10 drivers could compete in the Chase for the Cup.

The Chase is On!

The Sprint Cup is the top prize in NASCAR. The driver who earns the most points in a year wins. The last 10 races of the season are called the Chase for the Cup.

Jimmie Johnson, 2006 champion

The Chase begins after the first 26 races of the season. Most drivers can't even compete for the Cup. Only the 12 drivers with the most points can be in the Chase.

2006, Subway 500

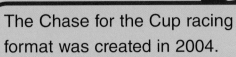

The top 12 drivers have their points reset at 5,000. They get bonus points for any races they won that season. Then drivers battle through 10 races.

Tony Stewart wins the 2007 Allstate 400.

15

Daytona Beach, 1958

16

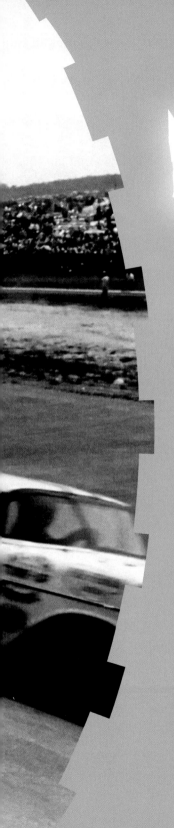

Not Quite Stock Cars

NASCAR racing is also called stock car racing. In the early days, drivers raced stock cars. They were the same cars that people drove on the streets.

roll cage

Over the years, changes were made
to the race cars. **Features** like roll cages
made cars safer. Special tires were added
for better handling.

feature — an important part of something

19

Today's race cars have no doors.
Drivers slide in through glassless
windows. There are no side mirrors
to slow the cars down, either.

glassless window

2352

DISCOUNT TIRE

21

NASCAR Points Champions

Driver	Year	Driver	Year	Driver	Year
Red Byron	1949	David Pearson	1969	Rusty Wallace	1989
Bill Rexford	1950	Bobby Isaac	1970	Dale Earnhardt	1990
Herb Thomas	1951	Richard Petty	1971	Dale Earnhardt	1991
Tim Flock	1952	Richard Petty	1972	Alan Kulwicki	1992
Herb Thomas	1953	Benny Parsons	1973	Dale Earnhardt	1993
Lee Petty	1954	Richard Petty	1974	Dale Earnhardt	1994
Tim Flock	1955	Richard Petty	1975	Jeff Gordon	1995
Buck Baker	1956	Cale Yarborough	1976	Terry Labonte	1996
Buck Baker	1957	Cale Yarborough	1977	Jeff Gordon	1997
Lee Petty	1958	Cale Yarborough	1978	Jeff Gordon	1998
Lee Petty	1959	Richard Petty	1979	Dale Jarrett	1999
Rex White	1960	Dale Earnhardt	1980	Bobby Labonte	2000
Ned Jarrett	1961	Darrell Waltrip	1981	Jeff Gordon	2001
Joe Weatherly	1962	Darrell Waltrip	1982	Tony Stewart	2002
Joe Weatherly	1963	Bobby Allison	1983	Matt Kenseth	2003
Richard Petty	1964	Terry Labonte	1984	Kurt Busch	2004
Ned Jarrett	1965	Darrell Waltrip	1985	Tony Stewart	2005
David Pearson	1966	Dale Earnhardt	1986	Jimmie Johnson	2006
Richard Petty	1967	Dale Earnhardt	1987		
David Pearson	1968	Bill Elliott	1988		

Cup Records

Some names stand out in the history of the Sprint Cup. Richard Petty's nickname is "The King." He was the first driver to win seven points championships.

Dale Earnhardt's nickname was "The Intimidator." He was the second driver to reach seven Cup victories. He and Petty are tied for the most points championships.

Dale Earnhardt

Petty and Earnhardt share a **record**. But Cale Yarborough did something neither of them could do. From 1976 to 1978, he won three championships in a row.

record — when something is done better than it has ever been done before

Jeff Gordon

Today, Jeff Gordon is closest to beating Petty and Earnhardt's record. But other drivers are right behind him. Anything can happen during the Chase for the Cup!

Glossary

feature (FEE-chuhr) — an important part or quality of something

qualify (KWAHL-uh-fye) — to earn a starting spot in a race by completing timed laps

record (REK-urd) — when something is done better than anyone has ever done it before

Sprint Cup (SPRINT CUP) — the championship held in NASCAR's top stock car racing series; from 2003 to 2007, it was called the Nextel Cup; from 1972 through 2003, it was called the Winston Cup; before 1972, it was known as the Grand National.

stock car (STOK CAR) — a car for racing, made from a regular model sold to the public

Read More

Buckley, James Jr. *NASCAR: Speedway Superstars.* Pleasantville, New York: Reader's Digest, 2004.

Gigliotti, Jim. *Fantastic Finishes: NASCAR's Great Races.* The World of NASCAR. Maple Plain, Minn.: Tradition Books, 2004.

Kelley, K. C. *Champions! of NASCAR.* All-Star Readers. Pleasantville, New York: Reader's Digest, 2005.

Internet Sites

FactHound offers a safe, fun way to find Internet sites related to this book. All of the sites on FactHound have been researched by our staff.

Here's how:
1. Visit *www.facthound.com*
2. Choose your grade level.
3. Type in this book ID **1429612851** for age-appropriate sites. You may also browse subjects by clicking on letters, or by clicking on pictures and words.
4. Click on the **Fetch It** button.

FactHound will fetch the best sites for you!

Index